While every precaution has been taken in the preparation of this book, the publisher assumes no responsibility for errors or omissions, or for damages resulting from the use of the information contained herein.

ENJOY THE STREET LIFE OF BANGKOK WITH THESE DISHES!: TAKE A COLORFUL AND FLAVORFUL TRIP THROUGH THE STREETS OF BANGKOK WITH THESE RECIPES

First edition. August 23, 2021.

Copyright © 2021 Ida Smith.

ISBN: 979-8201064211

Written by Ida Smith.

Table of Contents

Enjoy the Street Life of Bangkok with these Dishes!

Take a Colorful and Flavorful Trip through the Streets of Bangkok with these Recipes

BY: Ida Smith

License Notes

Introduction

From the right, left and centre of the Bangkok streets, sellers are calling your attention there to delicious dishes and drinks.

Talking about Iced Tea, Nam Matoom, Chuoi Chung, Kai Jeow, etc., these street food dishes and drinks are what makes Bangkok an enjoyable tourist destination.

Keep calm as we bring them to your kitchen.

Welcome to Bangkok, Thailand!!!

Recipe 1 - Gai Hor Bai Toey

This pandan leaf wrapped chicken tastes so glorious. Do you want to try it out?!!!

Prep time: 08 minutes

Cooking time: 18 minutes

Servings: 2

Ingredients

- 1 cup coriander/soy bean paste
- 200g chunked chicken fillet
- 1 teaspoon sesame oil
- 1 cup cooking oil
- 1 teaspoon sugar
- 1 dash dark soy sauce
- 1 tablespoon fish sauce

- 7 washed pandan leaves

Directions
Combine the paste, sugar, chicken fillet, sauces and sesame oil in a bowl. Mix well.
Scoop the marinated chicken fillet in the pandan leaves. Wrap to form cone shapes.
Deep fry the wrapped chicken in a pot of the oil.
Fry till the leaves turn dark green.
Transfer to a plate.
Serve.

Recipe 2 - Gaeng Massaman

You'd get hooked from the first taste of it!!

Prep time: 07 minutes
Cooking time: 25 minutes
Servings: 2
Ingredients

- 1 chopped red onion
- 2 handfuls toasted peanuts
- 1 pound chunked chicken thigh fillet
- 7oz coconut milk
- 1 tablespoon tamarind paste
- 3 tablespoons Massaman curry paste
- 1 teaspoon salt

- 1 cinnamon stick
- 1 pound peeled and quartered potatoes
- 3 bay leaves
- 1 tablespoon sugar
- Cooked rice to serve

Directions
Boil the coconut milk in a pot.
Stir in the curry paste before it boils. Mix well.
Throw in the chicken and peanuts.
Add the remaining ingredients. Cook till the potatoes are soft.
Serve with cooked rice.

Recipe 3 - Khao Neeo Mamuang

We are all for the stickiness and the tastes and textures that come with this dish because it is the real deal!!

Prep time: 10 minutes

Cooking time: 15 minutes

Servings: 2

Ingredients

- 1 cup water
- 1 cup short grain white rice
- 12 tablespoons white sugar
- 1 cup coconut milk
- 1 dash salt
- 1 cup tapioca starch sauce
- 1 teaspoon roasted sesame seeds

- 2 peeled sliced mangoes

Directions
Cook the rice in a pan.
Combine the salt, coconut milk and sugar in another pan. Boil for 3 minutes.
Add the cooked rice to the mixture.
Serve the sticky rice. Garnish with the mangoes.
Add a drizzle of the sauce and sesame seeds over the rice and mangoes.
Enjoy.

Recipe 4 - Flavored Chicken Wings

This is a finger licking recipe that will make you scramble for more servings!

Prep time: 06 minutes

Cooking time: 15 minutes

Servings: 2

Ingredients

- 1 cup sweet chili sauce
- 3 tablespoons tempura flour
- 1 pinch salt
- 1 tablespoon water
- 250g chicken wings
- 1 pinch ground pepper
- 2 cups olive oil

- 1 handful spring onions
- 1 sprinkle sesame seeds

Directions

Combine the chicken wings, pepper and salt in a bowl. Mix well and marinate.

Toss in the water and flour. Mix well.

Deep fry the coated chicken wings with the oil. Drain on a paper lined plate.

Coat in the sauce. Allow marinating for 10 minutes.

Garnish with the spring onions and sesame seeds. Serve.

Enjoy.

Recipe 5 - Thai Boat Noodle Soup

Row your boat round around your bowl!!

Prep time: 07 minutes
Cooking time: 10 minutes
Servings: 2
Ingredients

- 1 minced garlic clove
- 1 tablespoon canola oil
- 1oz chopped spinach
- 4oz pork balls
- 2 cups pork broth
- 1 handful chopped cilantro leaves
- 1 chopped celery stalk

- 2oz sliced pork meat
- 3oz soaked and drained flat rice noodles
- 1 tablespoon beef blood
- 1 handful bean sprouts
- 2 tablespoons Thai fish sauce
- 2 tablespoons granulated sugar
- 2 tablespoons chili powder
- 2 tablespoons sliced pickled Thai chilies

Directions

Boil the noodles, pork balls, pork meat and celery in a pot of the broth. Cook till softened.

Sauté the garlic in a pan of the oil.

Add the bean sprouts and spinach to the pot of the noodles.

Cook for 1 minute more.

Serve into bowls.

Top with the garlic oil and broth.

Add the blood to the bowls.

Garnish with the remaining ingredients.

Enjoy.

Recipe 6 - Nam Matoom

Either served cold or hot, this drink is not just aromatic but delicious!!

Prep time: 04 minutes
Cooking time: 06 minutes
Servings: 2
Ingredients

- 4 teaspoons sugar
- 2 cups water
- 1 cup sliced dried bael fruit

Directions
Boil the water for 2 minutes.
Add the bael fruit.

Toss in the sugar.
Cook and stir till all your sugar is dissolved.
Turn off the heat. Serve either chilled or hot.

Recipe 7 - Mango Iced Tea

This is heavenly citrusy excitement in a tall glass!!

Prep time: 03 minutes
Cooking time: 04 minutes
Servings: 2
Ingredients

- 2 cups water
- 1 cup raspberries
- 1 cup mango juice
- 2 black tea bags
- 1 cup sliced mango
- 1 tablespoon honey

Directions

Boil the tea bags with the water.
Add the honey and mango juice. Stir well.
Transfer the tea to a pitcher.
Add the mango.
Chill for 40 minutes.
Garnish with the raspberries and remaining mango (if you have any left). Serve.
Enjoy.

Recipe 8 - Cha Yen

Iced tea might taste the same everywhere, but on the streets of Bangkok, you're in for an explosive treat!!

Prep time: 07 minutes

Cooking time: 10 minutes

Servings: 1

Ingredients

- 8oz water
- 1 tablespoon red rooibos tea leaves
- 4 tablespoons half-and-half
- 1 tablespoon black tea leaves
- 1 teaspoon vanilla extract
- 5 cloves
- 5 chopped star anise pods

- 1 tablespoon granulated sugar
- 4 tablespoons condensed milk
- Ice cubes

Directions

Boil water in a pot. When it's boiled, turn off the heat and add the tea leaves, cloves, star anise pods and sugar.

Cover and allow steeping for 6 minutes.

Combine the vanilla extract, milk and half and half in a bowl. Mix well.

Strain your hot liquid into a chilled glass of ice.

Top with the milk mixture.

Enjoy.

Recipe 9 - Butterfly Pea with Lime

Purple is the new lemonade color!!

Prep time: 06 minutes
Cooking time: nil
Servings: 1
Ingredients

- 2 tablespoons elderflower syrup
- 7 tablespoons club soda
- 4 tablespoons butterfly pea flower tea
- 7 tablespoons lemon juice
- 2 lemon slices
- Ice cubes

Directions

Combine the syrup and lemon juice in a glass. Stir well.
Add ice to cover the lemon juice mixture.
Pour in the butterfly pea flower tea.
Top with the soda.
Garnish with the lemon slices.

Recipe 10 - Nam Manao

Limeade anyone?!!

Prep time: 04 minutes
Cooking time: 05 minutes
Servings: 2
Ingredients

- 8 tablespoons lime juice
- 1 dash salt
- 4 tablespoons sugar
- 1 cup water
- 1 handful lime slices
- 3 mint leaves

Directions
Boil the water till bubbling. Turn off the heat.
Add the salt and sugar. Stir to get them dissolved.
Add the lime slices. Keep aside to cool.
Stir in the lime juice. Chill.
Garnish with the mint leaves.
Serve.

Recipe 11 - Caramel Candy

From generation to generation, this delicious candy recipe has been on the streets of Bangkok!!

Prep time: 05 minutes
Cooking time: 15 minutes
Servings: 24
Ingredients

- 1 dash vanilla extract
- 5 tablespoons butter
- 10 tablespoons granulated sugar
- 4oz condescend milk
- 5 tablespoons light corn syrup

Directions
Combine the corn syrup, sugar, milk and butter in a microwave safe bowl.

Microwave for 15 minutes till the mixture is golden.
Remove from the microwave. Add in the vanilla extract. Mix well.
Transfer into a buttered rectangle pan. Chill.
Cut into candy forms and wrap up.
Serve immediately or store.

Recipe 12 - Fried Banana Pancakes

On the Bangkok streets, anything is possible!!! Fried Banana Pancakes are possible too!!!

Prep time: 10 minutes

Cooking time: 15 minutes

Servings: 8

Ingredients

- 4 peeled ripe bananas
- 2 cups olive oil
- 250g pancake mix
- 350ml milk
- 1 cup powdered sugar
- 1 teaspoon ground cinnamon

Directions

Smash the bananas in a bowl.

Add the milk, cinnamon and pancake mix. Whisk well.

Scoop the mixture into a pan of the oil. Fry till golden brown.

Add a garnish of the sugar over the hot pancakes.

Serve.

Enjoy.

Recipe 13 - Nam Bi Toey

Refreshing!

Prep time: 03 minutes
Cooking time: 05 minutes
Servings: 1
Ingredients

- 150g water
- 10g chopped pandan leaves
- 80g sugar

Directions

Blitz the pandan leaves and water till crushed.
Strain into a pan. Add the sugar and boil.

Serve cool.

Recipe 14 - Long Thailand Iced Tea Cocktail

This beautiful blend of beverage and cocktail would give you a thrilling taste of ..... bliss!!

Prep time: 10 minutes
Cooking time: nil
Servings: 2
Ingredients

- 2oz brandy
- 1oz hot water
- 1oz honey
- 2oz sweetened condensed milk
- 2oz dark rum
- 4oz club soda
- 2oz rye whiskey

- 4oz red Thai tea
- Ice cubes

Directions
Combine the water and honey in a shaker. Shake well to dissolve the honey.
Keep aside to cool.
Add the rum, brandy, whiskey, milk, tea and ice in the shaker. Shake well.
Strain into long glasses of ice.
Top with the soda. Enjoy.

Recipe 15 - Chuoi Chung

If we told you how delicious this dessert is, we wouldn't be helping you. You should taste it yourself.

Prep time: 06 minutes
Cooking time: 20 minutes
Servings: 2
Ingredients

- 15g boiled tapioca pearls
- 20g chopped and toasted hazelnuts
- 80g caster sugar
- 80g peeled and cubed cassava
- 1 large sliced sugar banana
- 200ml water
- 1 handful toasted sesame seeds
- 100ml sweetened coconut cream
- Salt to taste

Directions

Combine the sugar, coconut cream, cassava and water in a pot.

Cook till boiling.

Add the banana and tapioca pearls.

Cook till the banana is crushed.

Add salt.

Garnish with more coconut cream, sesame seeds and hazelnuts. Serve.

Recipe 16 - Moo Manao

Do you want your pork dish delicious, tender, crunchy and spicy and busting with flavors? This is a recipe to have handy!!

Prep time: 10 minutes
Cooking time: nil
Servings: 2
Ingredients

- 1 cup crunchy vegetables
- 300g blanched and thinly sliced pork loin
- 6 tablespoons water
- 4 tablespoons soy sauce
- 3 tablespoons palm sugar
- 4 tablespoons canola oil
- 3 Thai chilies

- 2 tablespoons cornstarch
- 4 tablespoons fish sauce
- 7 cilantro springs
- 6 tablespoons lime juice
- 5 garlic cloves
- 4 cups shredded cabbage
- 1 handful mint sprigs

Directions

Combine the soy sauce, pork loin, oil, cornstarch and water in a bowl. Keep aside for 30 Minutes.

Add the fish sauce, chilies, garlic, sugar and lime juice in the blender. Blitz to form a paste dressing. Add the cilantro springs to the paste. Mix well.

Arrange the cabbage on plates. Put the pork on it. Serve the dressing on it. Garnish with the mint sprigs, lime slices and veggies.

Enjoy.

Recipe 17 - Thab Thim Krob

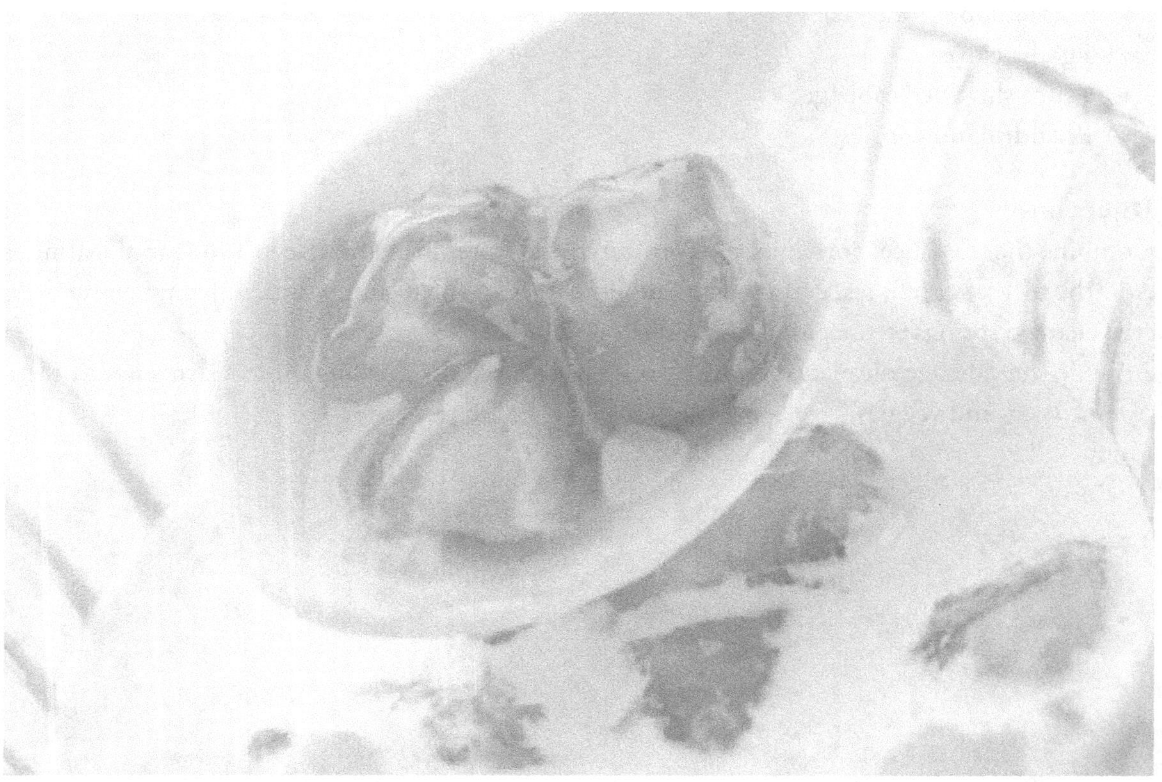

This is crunchy delightfulness!!

Prep time: 12 minutes
Cooking time: 10 minutes
Servings: 2
Ingredients

- 200g sugar
- 2oz tapioca flour
- 200ml water
- 1 dash red food coloring
- 300g peeled and chopped water chestnuts
- 200ml coconut milk

Directions

Boil the sugar and 150ml of the water in a pan.

Cook till a syrup is formed.

Add the coconut milk. Chill.

Put the water chestnuts in a bowl of water.

Add the red coloring.

Toss well.

Put the tapioca flour in a bowl.

Drain the water chestnuts and pour in the bowl of tapioca flour. Coat the water chestnuts in the flour.

Boil a pot of 50ml of the water. Spoon the coated water chestnuts into the boiling water.

Cook till floating. Spoon in to a bowl of cold water.

Add the coconut milk mixture to the water chestnuts.

Serve cold.

Recipe 18 - Oyster Omelet

This is for your love for oysters!!

Prep time: 06 minutes

Cooking time: 08 minutes

Servings: 1

Ingredients

- 1 cup sweet chili sauce
- 1 handful spring onions
- 2 beaten eggs
- 3 tablespoons canola oil
- 1 teaspoon Shaoxing wine
- 1 minced garlic clove
- 1 tablespoon salt

- 1 tablespoon fish sauce
- 6 shucked oysters
- 2 tablespoons sweet potato starch
- 50ml water
- 1 teaspoon rice flour

Directions

Mix the last three ingredients in a bowl.

Keep aside. Scoop the mixture into a pan of the oil. Scoop the eggs on top.

Cook and toss the content together.

Push to a part of the pan. Then, sauté the garlic in the space in the pan. Add in the oysters, wine, salt, fish sauce and spring onions.

Cook till done.

Toss everything together. Garnish with the chili sauce and serve.

Recipe 19 - Kai Jeow

Rather than the versions you might find in the western world, this Thai omelette is solid and mouthwatering!!

Prep time: 04 minutes

Cooking time: 06 minutes

Servings: 1

Ingredients

- 1 egg
- 2 handfuls ground pork meat
- 3 tablespoons canola oil
- 1 dash fish sauce
- 1 dash soy sauce

Directions
Whisk the egg, pork meat and sauces in a bowl. Mix well.
Fry the mixture in a pan of the oil.
Fry the omelette till both sides are done and crispy
Serve. Enjoy.

Recipe 20 - Deep Fried Insects

Hold on!! Don't freak out yet! You're going to freak out in excitement later, but that's after you've had a taste of this delicious but weird recipe!

Prep time: 10 minutes
Cooking time: 15 minutes
Servings: 2
Ingredients

- 3 cups mixed edible insects (worms, grasshoppers and crickets)
- 3 cups canola oil
- 1 tablespoon salt
- 3 tablespoons sweet ground chili
- 2 cups sweet soy sauce

Directions
Clean and wash the insects well.
Pat dry. Marinate in the salt.
Fry in a pan of the oil.
Garnish with the chili and soy sauce. Serve. Enjoy.

Recipe 21 - Coconut Ice Cream

If you're a lover of a creamy coconut taste, this recipe will never disappoint you!!

Prep time: 10 minutes

Cooking time: nil

Servings: 4

Ingredients

- 7oz coconut cream
- 8 tablespoons milk
- 12 tablespoons sweetened coconut flakes
- 12 tablespoons heavy cream

Directions

Mix the coconut cream and milk in the processor.

Pulse till well mixed.
Add the heavy cream and coconut flakes.
Pour into a bowl.
Chill till you're ready to serve.

Recipe 22 - Khanom Buang

This dessert looks like your regular tacos but tastes deliciously different.

Prep time: 15 minutes

Cooking time: 10 minutes

Servings: 4

Ingredients

- 1 tablespoon crushed egg shell
- 60ml water
- 40g rice flour
- 70g sugar
- 1 dash cocoa powder
- 15g mung bean flour
- 3 tablespoons foi thong

- 1 medium egg
- 2 egg whites
- 3 tablespoons sugar

Directions

Add the water and egg shell to a bowl. Keep aside.

Combine 3 tablespoons of the sugar and egg whites in a bowl. Whisk well.

Scoop the egg shell water into a bowl. Add 70g of the sugar, the bean flour, egg, rice flour and cocoa powder. Mix well.

Scoop the flour mixture into a heated pan in a circular motion. Cook for 15 seconds before spooning the egg white mixture and foi thong on it in the middle.

Cook till the batter is light brown and crispy.

Serve.

Recipe 23 - Chicken and Cashew

Heavenly!!

Prep time: 08 minutes
Cooking time: 15 minutes
Servings: 2
Ingredients

- 1 cup dark fish sauce
- 1 lengthwise sliced green onion
- 1 tablespoon peanut oil
- 2 halved and seeded dried red chilies
- 1 minced garlic clove
- 1 handful toasted cashew nuts
- 1 handful quartered yellow onion

- 4oz chunked chicken breast
- Cooked rice to serve

Directions
Sauté the red chilies, yellow onion and garlic in a pan of the oil.
Toss in the chicken and cashew nuts.
Add the sauce. Toss well.
Garnish with the green onion.
Serve with cooked rice.
Enjoy.

Recipe 24 - Som Tam

This sweet combination of crunchiness, sweetness, spiciness and tartness will blow your palate away!!!

Prep time: 40 minutes
Cooking time: nil
Servings: 8
Ingredients

- 6 lengthwise sliced scallions
- 1 cup roasted nuts
- 4 cups bean sprouts
- 1 tablespoon granulated sugar
- 8 tablespoons chopped Thai basil
- 2 cups halved cherry tomatoes
- 4 tablespoons vegetable oil
- 10 large sliced green beans

- 4 tablespoons brown sugar
- 6 tablespoons lemon juice
- 4 tablespoons fish sauce
- 2 minced garlic cloves
- 2 unripe peeled and grated green papaya
- 2 chopped seeded red chili pepper

Directions

Process the sauce, lemon juice, chili pepper, garlic, oil and sugars in the processor to get your dressing.
Bruise the green beans lightly in a chopper.
Combine the papaya, bean sprouts, basil, green beans and tomatoes in a large bowl.
Toss in the dressing.
Add the nuts.
Serve with the scallions.

Recipe 25 - Khanom Tom

Let's introduce you to a special version of coconut that you never thought existed!!

Only on Bangkok streets!!

Prep time: 08 minutes

Cooking time: 10 minutes

Servings: 10

Ingredients

- 10 tablespoons glutinous rice flour
- 9 tablespoons water
- 3 tablespoons palm sugar syrup
- 1 cup shredded coconut

Directions

Pour the syrup into a pan. Stir in 8 tablespoons of the coconut. Cook till the mixture is caramelized. Mix the water and rice flour in a bowl to form a soft dough.

Cover and keep aside for a while.

On a floured surface, roll the coconut mixture into balls. Place the balls into chunks. Wrap them up to form round dumplings.

Cook the dumplings in a pot of water till they float. Transfer to a plate.

Coat the balls in a bowl of the leftover coconut.

Serve and enjoy.

Recipe 26 - Lemon Tea

Soothingly addictive and refreshing!!

Prep time: 03 minutes
Cooking time: 04 minutes
Servings: 1
Ingredients

- 1 tablespoon honey
- 1 tablespoon black tea leaves
- 1 cup water
- 1 tablespoon lemon juice

Directions
Boil the water till simmering.

Add the black tea leaves. Cover to allow simmering.
Strain into your teacup. Stir in the honey and lemon juice.
Enjoy.

Recipe 27 - Nom Yen

Refreshingly creamy and sweet!!

Prep time: 07 minutes
Cooking time: nil
Servings: 1
Ingredients

- 1 cup milk
- 3 tablespoons evaporated milk
- 2 cups crushed ice
- 3 tablespoons sala flavoured syrup

Directions
Combine the syrup and milk in a jar.

Add the crushed ice. Stir well.
Add a drizzle of the evaporated milk.
Enjoy.

Recipe 28 - Pla Pao

Coated in a salt crust, this grilled fish is one of the most delicious dishes we have tasted. And that's all truth!!

Prep time: 10 minutes
Cooking time: 1 hour
Servings: 1
Ingredients

- 2 cups Thai seafood sauce
- 1kg salt
- 2 full whole fishes
- 1 handful lime leaves
- 1 tablespoon water
- 3 tablespoons flour

- 3 lemongrass stalks

Directions
Clean the fishes. Remove the guts. Wash the fishes. But don't slice the fishes up.
Crumble the lemongrass stalks with a rolling pin.
Stuff the fishes with the lime leaves and lemongrass stalks.
Combine the flour, water and salt in a bowl. Mix well.
Coat the fishes with the mixture.
Grill the coated fishes till firm.
Serve with the seafood sauce

Recipe 29 - Green Curry Chicken

Toss in coconut milk, carrots, some spices and some other ingredients to get a serving of this delicious state of the art dish.

Prep time: 07 minutes
Cooking time: 15 minutes
Servings: 3
Ingredients

- 1 pound diced chicken breast
- 1 tablespoon coconut oil
- 7oz coconut milk
- 1 tablespoon minced ginger
- 1 small diced yellow onion
- 2 minced garlic cloves
- 1 dash cilantro

- 6 tablespoons Thai green curry paste
- 1 tablespoon granulated sugar
- 1 medium diced zucchini
- 1 cup shredded carrots
- 1 dash chopped basil
- 1 tablespoon lime juice
- 1 pinch black pepper
- 1 dash salt

Directions
Sauté the onion in a pan of the oil.
Throw in the chicken. Cook till done.
Toss in the spices, curry paste, coconut milk, sugar, carrots, pepper and zucchini.
Throw in the cilantro and the remaining ingredients.
Serve.

Recipe 30 - Tom Yum

Are you sure that you are ready for all the excitement and addictiveness that this soup is bringing?
Are you??!

Prep time: 07 minutes
Cooking time: 12 minutes
Servings: 1
Ingredients

- 1 cup shrimp stock
- 200g tail on shrimp
- 1 galangal slice
- 3 chopped oyster mushrooms
- 3 bruised kaffir lime leaves
- 3 pounded bird's eyes chilies

- 2 tablespoons fish sauce
- 1 tablespoon nam prik pao oil
- 1 tablespoon roasted Thai chili paste
- 2 tablespoons lime juice
- 1 pounded lemongrass stalk
- Cilantro for garnishing

Directions
Add the stock in a pot. Toss in everything else.
Boil till the shrimp is cooked.
Serve. Garnish with cilantro.

Conclusion

From Soi Cowboy Street to Sukhumvit Road, Khao San Road, Royal City Avenue, etc., all through the streets of Bangkok, there are appealing street food dishes and drinks that you can't resist trying, no matter how hard you try!

But instead of going from one street to another trying out these street food dishes and drinks, we have brought them home to you in this cookbook.

So, take a culinary trip through the streets of Bangkok with the cookbook.

Bon Culinary Voyage!!

Don't miss out!

Visit the website below and you can sign up to receive emails whenever Ida Smith publishes a new book. There's no charge and no obligation.

https://books2read.com/r/B-A-LRXL-EILRB

BOOKS2READ

Connecting independent readers to independent writers.